CASTAWAY

by
Katherine Riegel

FutureCycle Press
futurecycle.org

CASTAWAY

Copyright 2010 Katherine Riegel
All Rights Reserved

Published by FutureCycle Press
Cave Spring, Georgia, U.S.A.

ISBN: 978-0-9828612-5-7

For Ira

CONTENTS

I

II

III

IV

V

I

PARADISE LOST: ONE

The back yard rose
from the house to the barn
like an uncrested wave we rode up
and down daily, in all weather. Summer
was the best, a piece of black
vinyl laid out with a hose blasting cold
well water across it and then, for a winged moment,
speed and grace and laughter. I lost
the tiny silver leaf
from my favorite ring
in the mud at the bottom of that sweet slope,
but my mother said, "It's just
a *thing*" and I ran back
to the top, seal-slick and ready
to slide down again. Oh

ocean-swell of home, how
would I ever find my sea legs
once I had to sail away from you?

AMBROSIA

They say we have finished becoming
by age seven. We are
the tree in the front yard
by then—drag queen spectacle at Christmas,
pale fingered in the spring,
dark like green secrets in the summer—
but never any different bark, leaves
of another species, arms the shape of castle spires.

I am still looking for that ordinary key
to open the door in the hedge, the not-real
reaching up into my world, waiting to be tripped over.
I still cherish the number 6:
the number of people in my family,
the number of shelves in the upstairs bookcases
which I counted again and again as I sat in the hall
between my room and my parents',
the family sleeping,
my leg muscles writhing like demons beneath me.

Once upon a time a sick child wept
when her mother sang *My bonnie*
lies over the ocean. She wept and could not
stop, she wept until the whole house
filled with salty water,
the people and the beds and all
the objects of belonging floating near the ceiling,
and still the song continued:
Oh bring back my bonnie to me.

The children's chewable aspirin tasted
like ambrosia, and sometimes
I found it myself and ate more than one
and then crawled back to bed
no one else awake.

When I confessed
in the morning I could never tell
whether I had done right,
so the next time I woke my mother,
and she gave me one orange tablet
and rubbed my legs until I slept.

CHILDHOOD: A PORTRAIT

A quiet child in a still room. Each undusted surface as mysterious
as a deep sea creature. Slow time and nothing
to measure it—no small sounds, even her breathing muted.
How to explain this curious moment? Vision
is there, hearing, smell, taste, touch. But all
is removed, distant. Outside the trees
are in full leaf. The sun pulls matter to itself and breathes.
In this moment there must
be secret doors to other worlds. There must
be others. She feels the tiniest flecks fall
against her face and rest there, the pump
of her heart like a furnace she cannot help but stoke.
She does not move. The world
does not move around her. Downstairs everyone
is frozen, like in that children's game
where you go wild for a minute, then stop
just where you are.

Do not ask
what she is waiting for, what purpose the white, deep quiet.
You know yourself
what wounds is the same
for all of us.

In Illinois, Everything Breathes

Our front porch faced north,
my mother told me. We watched
heavy cloud banks sweep in, trailing funnels
like lethal tails. The wind brought
the urgent smell of rain
                                        and a sure answering
wildness in me, an unseen buffeting
hawk in too small a cage. My mother
waited until duty to my father's fear
finally sent us inside, under the stairs—
which I liked, too, the whole family crouched
together in that close windowless closet,
the radio's calm prophecies marking
neighboring towns and counties and sometimes
our own.
                    When the radio said it was safe
we burst from the stifling heart of the house
and ran out breathless through its open mouth.

ART

I was the worst artist
in my third grade class.
My sculpture project was a lopsided
pot with a handle, decorated around the rim
with clay pebbles the size and shape of my thumb tip
into which I'd carved smiley faces with a toothpick.
The teacher's smile
was both bemused and patronizing. How could
a girl so smart have so little
aesthetic sense? When we got back
our projects from the kiln where they'd been
fired into permanence, I knew
how pathetic mine was. Besides
the ungainly and impractical design (some
of the pebble-faces had fallen off
in the oven) the blue paint
I had chosen looked dripped on, and not
charmingly. It was supposed to be
rich and glossy, but on my pot
it was weak and thin, a faint sheen in places
and completely bare in others.
I had wanted to give it to my mother,
to believe it might emerge from the heat
improved beyond recognition. Instead I
clutched that pot to myself in shame, looked with envy
on the elegant dove my tablemate held
(in a pink that matched the fringe
of her fabric-covered notebook) and turned
my back on my own artistic versatility.
But I didn't throw it out. I couldn't.
It was ugly and heavy, a failed making,
but those smiley blobs of clay
spoke in my voice. They couldn't help
I hadn't the skill to give them
something beautiful to say.

NAGA

*"Ts! Ts!" said Kaa, weaving his head to and fro. "I also have
known what love is."*
—Rudyard Kipling, The Jungle Book

We rode serpentines in the dust
of the arena, training both rider
and horse in the art of bending.
I never thought then of
snakes, the silky creatures I found
fascinating and my sister loathed.
I didn't think of symbols, either,
ancient shapes meaning
protection, healing, immortality, nor
of inevitable encounters
with the serpents hiding
behind zippers, like all snakes
preferring private places.

And when I mowed
the lower pasture, my sweat
coalescing in the breeze, the tractor
rumbling beneath me, I didn't worry
for the poor garter snakes under the long grass
(though I do now, those maligned
and thankless animals whose voracious
appetite for grasshoppers and June bugs—my own
phobic plagues—serve us so well). No,

I just got bored
with straight lines, big and little
boxes, so I turned and turned the wheel,
making serpentines with grassy scales,
great looping serpents swallowing their own tails
over and over under the sacred sky.

ASK ME WHAT SUMMER MEANS

July nights held their breath
when we played flashlight tag, a game of
wisdom and the deeper mysteries. That kind of dark

filled the mouth, like the heavy air we
panted in and out after a hard run
back to the tree we used as base.
Once I lay down
under the bushes with Colby Bowman—two years
older and way

out of my league—but he touched
my hair, rested his arm
casually across my back.
Flashlight tag was never about knowing
anything—it was about stillness and glorious
release. *Ollyollyincomefree* brought most of us
running, sneakers slapping the ground, arms
pinwheeling, like ducks taking off from a pond.

Sometimes a couple just breaking
into the teens—usually my older brother and
the newest neighbor girl in a tube top—
stayed hidden through two rounds,
straggled in eventually with grass
in their hair. The cicada's song of desire
was with us all, our sweat as intoxicating

as pixie dust. Little Katydid was the youngest,
and she was shrewd, knowing every hiding place
in bounds. Once she hid too well and the others
went off, forgetting her, to tell ghost stories in the barn.

No matter. There were books inside
with covers that creaked open like doors.

Scheisse, I would have said, if I had known
that word then. *You are all scheisse.*
But I played again the next night,
and the next, pelting blindly into the throat
of another Illinois summer.

GREEN VELVET

My brother ate a moth
at a party once.
He described the fluttering
of the dry wings
in his throat.
This moth
would never have been a bird's meal,
trapped as it was,
inside. Still,
something of the natural order of things
was disturbed that night—
no light flickering
in my brother's stomach,
nothing to hold the moth
enthralled during its long
esophageal journey.

Last night I dreamt my brother
wore women's clothes, like
when we were kids
and he had to baby-sit
us, his siblings younger by five and seven years.
Putting on our mother's dress
and bra stuffed with socks
he became "Mama Mia,"
a clown in falsetto.
I doubt his own children
would giggle as we did,
seeing his bony knees protrude
under green velvet.
There are some things
a brother can do that a father cannot.

LETTER TO A CHILD WITH A LUCKY CLOVER COLLECTION

Oh, my diffident child,
you are not safe.
The birds in their leaves,
the haughty dogs snapping at tails
of automobile exhaust, the raccoons
answering siren songs of rubber–
they are in the hole
of their mothers' hearts
compared to you.

You are endangered by the very sun.
You will feel locusts swarming
behind your eyes in some city
in some year your boots are stuck in
and you will not be able to escape
in your sock feet through the mud.

And if you hide in the feedbox
in the dusty warm smell of grain
in the coffined darkness
you will not be found
and you will still
be lifted up
and taken into the grass
and impaled on memory
so sharp no four-leaf clover can save you.

MY FATHER IN ILLINOIS

His hands are effete, worried,
vaguely incompetent,
but he is building the inside of a barn
for horses, spacious stalls
with double-hung doors so balanced
a child will open and close them easily
all her life
until she is ten and has to leave.
For him, this place is a desert island
on which he is marooned. Around him the flat,
becalmed fields, too open to the sky.
No hills, no trees, no cold, sweet streams.
He must work, or die.

I want to know
how he could not love
this farm, this barn
with its good strong wood
that he precisely cut and nailed,
the beams and rafters becoming
the frame of the ship I sail in dreams
ever after.
He lets the tape measure swallow itself
and looks down the dim aisle
towards the future me.
"It's not Pennsylvania," he says,
and both of us, forever castaways,
turn to our separate endeavors.

A FAIRY TALE OR NO

My mother looks back
out the window of the old blue station wagon

and the freshly painted house, the aluminum-sided barn and arena,
the upper and lower pastures, the wild area with its flowering hawthorns
disappear.

The year is 1979. She is only 43. There is fear
of oil shortages and gas rationing. My father works
in town half an hour away. He is unhappy. He
hates open, flat spaces. He likes towns.

The year is 1979. We are all worked to the bitter bone,
packing and loading and moving. When we arrive, more work—picking
        the stones
out of a small yard and raking, raking
so the sod can be put down. Bitter. But my mother
is working so her heart—
that flowered thing—
can't realize it's been picked.

The year is the same year.
It is always that year. The pivot. The axis
on which all our lives turn. Did my father become happy?
Did my mother die of this loss? Did I sputter and choke
in the fumes of the city? Did my sister forget
the smell of horseflesh and go off to college a new,
suburban coed, confident and savvy?

It is still 1979. How much work
to convince me and my brother, pre-pubescent and still
innocent, that what was coming would be an adventure.
I am ten again

and this time I say No. I say

You go ahead. Mom stays. I stay. My sister
stays, and avoids the kind of darkness
that waits for her. My brothers choose—both stay.
My father goes off to town, taking his unhappiness
like a path of sharp stones. We grow up.
The hawthorns flower. My mother
lives there still.

II

WHAT I KNEW

Cross country skiing with my mother and sister
took me down wooded paths
I knew from the humid
summer, long stretches beside the river
somnolent and half-frozen, through gardens
of ice like glass sculptures.
We breathed through our scarves,
the air smelling of damp wool.
Sometimes I found a small hill
and took it again and again. Once we got lost,
turned around in the big park, and as dusk
came on we watched deer
like ghosts pass us on
both sides, silent, and moving fast without
looking like they were making
any effort. I was eleven, my sister eighteen,
my mother still that indeterminate age
kids always assign to parents.
We stopped, breathed. We were not
afraid. We had only just moved
to town; what we still thought of
as our home had been a farm,
with plenty of winter nights outside
in the snowy dark. My mother
hesitated, unsure. My sister had little
sense of direction. I looked around
at the snow-quiet woods, the orange
of the Illinois sunset, the soothing
lack of human signs. I knew what
we were trying to get back to.
"This way," I said.

I broke my tailbone sledding
down the only hill for miles,
a miniature mound of snow shoved up
by the plow clearing the court
in front of my friend's condominium.
We were thirteen and bored
of listening to the Top 40, fantasizing
about boys under the poster of Leif Garrett
on her wall. For years his 1970s
face framed by feathered blonde hair
came to mind when I heard anyone
speak of Vikings, Leif Ericson no longer
the one who discovered America nearly
five centuries before Columbus but
a pop singer with a mouth that looked magic
to pre-teens.
                        So when the saucer sled
hit the ice-covered concrete after a quick
five-foot drop and I felt that ache,
I thought nothing
at first, just relieved
to be outside where my sporty
body was at ease, unmade-up,
dressed in sturdy jeans and boots.
I had to carry a pillow
to school for six weeks after that,
mercifully not an inflated hemorrhoid donut
but a foam rectangle with a faded blue
flowered case. My humiliation only made me
more alone. My friend advanced in the one subject
I did not know if I wanted to master:
being a girl, with all the blue eye-shadow
and awkward wooden clogs that entailed.
I learned pain both limits and frees us,
and that it hurt most when I stood up,

the agony like the shriek
when you first wrench open a stuck door,
and then the pain going on
like the creaking hinges
of that same door
finally opening or falling completely
shut.

THE SAME COIN

My brother invited me
to go out with him and his friends, a year
older and high-school normal:
they drank, sat around in the dark
recounting rock concerts and calling each other
names, drove from Denny's to someone's
house to the school parking lot as if
they were going somewhere.
I imagined being with them was like
being trapped in a car with ferrets, vaguely
unpleasant, unpredictable, and without language.

     I loved language then like a child, knowing only
     some if it—its cadences on the page of a book, its galloping
     horsiness, meaning with grace.
     I didn't know how other people used it, how, broken,
     it conveyed need and hope, too. I didn't

go. Instead my brother and his friends met
my best friend and then you
and at fifteen you discovered
what she had learned that semester in Jamaica, more than
1600 miles from the cradle of Illinois cornfields.
When you told me the next week, in the chaos
of the choir room, you said, "Why didn't you
come out that night? I thought you
were going to be there." You were
very brave, and as kind as you could be. You tried
to touch me, but my face was a closed door.
I didn't blame you. I hated
myself for my fear and arrogance. I understood
my friend was punishing me. She was going back to Jamaica
and I wasn't and now she had gone somewhere else
I hadn't. You would have to wait years

for me, and I would be restless then and even more afraid.
I'm sorry I didn't go
that night. I'm sorry I was always looking
for some other kind of language,
though the one our lips invented when we kissed
was sweet. I'm sorry I wanted
to throw high school so far away it would be
a worthless coin on the bottom of the ocean.
If I had gone,

would I have been your first? You said,
"I wish it had been you." And I wish
I knew less about leaving—that it is always
forever, that you cannot pluck
the same coin back out of the water.

HOW I WISH IT HAD BEEN

The back of a big car on a July night, kissing
some sweet-lipped college boy
like it was illegal
while that pulse beat in parts of me
I could barely name and certainly
couldn't have spoken aloud
to anyone. Our mouths &
tongues talkin' stars, talkin' poetry,
a green smell all around.
His hands delicately pushing
my collar back so he could taste
the curve where neck and shoulder meet.
Hours of this, and words
floating between us, warm.
And then, finally, another warmth, and a rhythm
so slow I couldn't stop
breathing. Moonlight
in my hair and his.
And that first crescendo
roaring out the windows and across
the fields.
Afterwards,
laughter, wind,
the long sleepy drive home.

ALL MY SINS

My sins live
in a high school cafeteria.
The young ones aren't quite sure where they are yet,
they're wondering if they belong here at all;
they have a fresh-picked look, they are
nerdy in their innocence, they have so much to learn
in the school of guilt. Of course

some of the new ones
come in older than they seem, knowing more, wanting to hang out
with the cool kids: those who had sex
in the front seat of a car on a residential street at 3am,
who wore a tight
mini-skirt and no underwear to a bar, casually
mentioning this to a married guy just before
he threw a dart that totally missed
the target, the leather-jacketed punk who smoked
cigars in the garage with the boys just to
piss off the host's controlling wife. Sluts and partiers,
all of them. We know where they stand—
in the back, nearest the windows, always half a step
from blowing this joint.

The earnest sit together as if at a study group,
telling themselves over and over again: I did not walk
my depressed student down to the health center
to see a counselor;
I never returned the book an acquaintance lent me, it sits
surrounded by shame on my bookshelf even now.

The oldest ones have been there long enough
to get bitter, to go through the stages
of rationalization and denial—Yeah, I rode on
when my brother said, Wait!
and didn't notice he was not following until

he appeared an hour later, pushing his bike while the chain
drooped uselessly, but he
was always tricking me
into slowing down so he could go sailing past.
How was I to know this time
he was in real trouble?

Worst of all are the lies, sitting at an island table no one will approach,
playing chess. Where were you
when I called? one asks, and the other snickers,
I was getting my hair cut, while she moves the knight
like a knife across the board. Another mutters,
Thinking? Oh, nothing. I was just
thinking about the moon.

It's getting kind of crowded in there
after all these years, and nobody ever eats.
I want to give them
some other kind of future, free them
from the oppressive puke green walls
and the clocks that are always wrong,
let them go live out their lives in some
college town somewhere
that's just interesting enough
to make you never want to leave but not
so challenging you can never rest,

but I admit
I don't want to meet
any of them some day
on the sidewalk, walking
a dog or carrying a laptop, and have to stop,
and talk, and hear their answers
to the question, So, what are you up to
these days?

GOSSIP

I thought I didn't want to know
what one person said to another in the dark.
I guess I never mastered the fine art
of hanging around—doing nothing much, but not
looking like it—which is when
most gossip happens, when someone mentions, as if
casually, that girl X is planning revenge
because girl Y a) called her a name (bitch, slut, whore, feminist)
b) flirted with guy Z (who is not but should be
going out with girl X) c) humiliated her in some
intentional or unintentional way.
I'd ruin the mood, anyway, my feigned
nonchalance falling away in a barrage of questions
and unsolicited opinions (Z's not worth it—
someone who talks that way about animals
can't be any kind of decent).
I found out last
and too late
which of my graduate school classmates
had slept with which of our teachers—
if I had known, I might have been brave enough
to let myself be seduced
by the man who told me the scratch
on my chin was sexy, whose poetry
devoured what was inside me
with its talk of mountains and fires and slipping out
of your body.
                   Maybe all those
who never told me anything thought I was
somehow above taking pleasure
in others' shame. Maybe I was too often
the object of gossip, should have been ashamed
myself, though I rarely was—don't
ask, it was always
about who and when I loved. As it is

always, which is why
I always want to know: love and sex, those deep mysteries,
can only be made sense of
over long distances
when the details are passed
mouth to mouth to mouth.

DIE FLEDERMAUS

for Andy

It was surely no coincidence, you say,
that your downfall occurred during a Wagner
opera. I imagine you with a girl,
the music's swelling melodrama,
your delicate heart tying itself round
with the desire to be petty
while she explained that "it was impossible."

But it was your own restlessness,
a drastic result of your fidgety nature,
how you fiddled with a string
on your ill-fitting sportcoat, slid
the mini-file from your pocket nail clippers
in a poorly planned effort
to saw through the offending thread,
and proceeded to stab yourself—
seven stitches worth—in the palm.

Still you were nearly oblivious,
held a tissue to the wound, tried to interest yourself
in the staged players; though even at nineteen
you knew Wagner was ruined for you.
Finally you confessed to the usher
and had to be led out, bleeding.

It is so much more difficult to bear
when we hurt ourselves publicly,
the shame no accident,
the accident no explanation.
Somehow I cannot keep this scene in my mind,
lock it away instead in my own opaqued files,
places where a pleasant fog
smothers embarrassment. Always except at night

I can keep my banes away from me;
then I fight the same battles
with varying characters and outcomes
like a storyteller trying out endings.

So when I tease you
for being "rootchy"—a Pennsylvania Dutch term
I learned in my father's parents' house—
I do not think of your poor mutilated hand,
the trail of red across the plush theater carpet;

I think of my grandmother Christabelle,
what she lost so early in the gray landscape
of her diseased brain, how my grandfather
sat with her every day for seven years,
how her worries led him to the most suffering I have seen.

Sometimes in my dreams you are lunging
against the end of a chain. Sometimes
we are looking at a picture
of a woman wearing a velvet choker
with a diamond pendant.
Sometimes I think it *was* a girl.
So much can happen in the dark,
among Wagner's unreal strains
and the blind, warm-blooded pulse of wings.

APOLOGY TO MY EXES

To a man, I left
you because someone hurt a younger
me in a particular way, and under all the
layers of shellac and plaster-of-Paris she lives
still. I seduced you
with smiles & eyes & breasts
promising frank girl-next-door-sweetness with
uninhibited sex. But for her
love came in a barbed wire
suit, and before you knew it
she had wrapped us
in cotton & gauze so we could not feel
anymore. I told you
it was your drinking or
your arrogance or the way you
shushed me during sports on tv, that you
didn't get my poetry, that we were too
different, too much
the same.
                    Forgive
that little girl, cruelly
trained in the art of going
numb. Forgive my too-logical
explanations. I loved
you, even your dangerous
bodies, the softness just inside
those hard man hips. I left you at the height
of our intimacy, running to another
room and locking the door behind me.
It was because
I loved you, because
I could still hear
your breathing, confused &
stunned, on the other
side, that I could never
open that door again.

AND OF THE SILENT HERO

Any day now,
the vines will sag along the fence,
the smoke-frost will oppress the garden,
some of the singers of the air will go.
If you had any summer fantasies
they are fading now, midsummer
long past, wights and other ghosts
condemned to clatter together like dried gourds.

It is terrible
to ache for what you have never had,
to roll over and over
in your never-cool sheets
and wish you dreamt in black and white,
while the sullen lightning
writes profundities in the sky
and your favorite color, green,
curls up like leaves in your mouth.

Valentino died
at thirty-one.
They said he was too effeminate,
so he arranged a boxing match
and knocked down a champ
and then died with poisonous blood spitting from his stomach.
Eighty-thousand mourners
rioted at his funeral.

The night before the match
you are in the car with him,
you are darkly beautiful,
you and he are everything to each other.
You tell him not to do it.
He drives slowly to a quiet park.
His hands express a hopelessness

as he gathers your hair in them;
the fireflies are foretelling winter;
you drink champagne from flutes in the glovebox;
what his eyes ask for
only you can give him.

GEOGRAPHY

Flat against the angled wall of the day,
I recall *velocity* and *drag*
and other useful terms from high school science.
It's all about the essential force
of solitude, the way a truck
bangs down the tar road
towards the river
and I stay curled
in the green house
that once was mine, in the hard half-truth
of a child's ownership—that whatever
one has can always be taken away.
A little step and turn
and I touch the wire surrounding the pasture,
though it lacks the electricity
that used to shock me into my own body. Now
the geography of this place—
front door facing squarely north—
slips and crashes to the floor, a picture
I tried to hang but lost my grip.

GRASS

If my parents were trees
their leaves would speak in different languages.
Their bodies would lean towards each other
and away, their twig-fingers would sometimes touch and grasp,
even twine around each other, vine-like, until in the winter
one became too brittle and broke
its hold. If my whole family—
me and my two brothers,
and my sister, the oldest—were green
living things, you would hear
a babble of voices in the wind.
You would hear us clamoring for shade
or sun, complaining there was
too much of both. You would know
when one of us sickened, grew pale.
There would be a stillness, a great
indrawn breath. And I would not
run away like the grass (covering huge
distances, hungering for that original
Midwest sea of prairie)
no matter how much I might want to.

III

THE ANGER SUIT

Our father comes over
to our mother's house
and they argue about money—some of it
sticking out of the washing machine lid,
moving like carrots being eaten
from underneath. Our father's rage
builds, the solid floor and doorframes
dissolving into it. But this time he says,
I've got to get my anger suit, and he puts on
a huge padded muffling thing.
He hits the washing machine,
the walls, and finally, our mother.
She is not harmed at first—
we think this is a splendid idea—she even laughs
a little at the spectacle he is:
huge Easter bunny, giant knee rolled in Ace bandages,
furious but nearly helpless, until
he pushes her too hard
and she falls backwards onto the linoleum.

We are stunned
for a moment, looking at each other—
the children we were and who we are now—
and then we push him back, stepping carefully
over our mother. We hit him, pummeling the thick soft
fabric, each contact a distant explosion, a once-fixed star
popping softly and winking out,
and we know, at once, and pause together,
the anger suit was for us all along.

HOW TO FOLLOW THE RULES

Grow up good. Learn from your older siblings' flagrant
mistakes, observe the scenes, the fights, your parents'
disappointment. When they ask you
why you aren't a typical adolescent, answer
you were just born that way. Angels
get gifts and love. Everyone

falls in love with you, and you need
everyone to. You can't help
the way love runs into a muddy
tributary and stalls, becomes stagnant, until
you can't get out except by leaving
that river for another. Go to school, but

seek balance. Don't let anyone accuse you
of too much anything. Write poems,
but go to law school. Drop out
quietly; even this will not be seen
as failure or eccentricity because you
never do anything without reason, because

you never yelled or broke down or tried
to kill yourself like some of those other
desperate souls you knew. Let pain
crumple into a ball no one could read
even if they could smooth it out again.
Smile self-deprecatingly when told

your picture should be next to *well-adjusted*
in the dictionary. Plan indiscretions
carefully to coincide with alcohol.
Sleep through mornings that show
your one dull path, the one you think
you've made for yourself and can't

remake, the one you plod down like an
old horse with blinders on who can smell
the wide world out there but doesn't remember
the jittery foal inside, the filly damn-fool-stupid
who raced across tender spring grass
just for the sake of the wind.

PRAYER TO BUDDHA FOR A GOOD JOURNEY

This woman will travel to Thailand
with her soon-to-be-husband, an American
with Thai parents. During the 18 hours
in the plane flying across the Pacific,
she will fiddle with the air vent over her head,
read, sleep quietly in the seat, keep
her humor with her like a pillow.
When she disembarks
into the oozing heat of Bangkok
her body will adjust, blood vessels rising
to the surface of her skin,
cooled blood moving through her flesh
efficiently, no soggy fat to slow and heat it.
She will understand her new relatives' modified English,
read the clues of culture like—well, not quite
like a native, like the *farang* she is, but at least
an astute white foreigner. In taxis
on the streets of Bangkok and Chiang Mai
she will learn to look
at the faces of her companions, turning
towards the outside only when a great
temple or market is pointed out to her,
so she will not see the dogs rooting through piles
of garbage like emaciated pigs.
She will have planned well enough—bug spray,
sunscreen, bottled water, toilet paper—
that the accumulated discomforts of travel
will not tire her, weigh down her legs, blister
her feet. She will see everything Thai
and beautiful: slender Buddhas in stone
and jade and gold, venerable temples,
and, from a train window, she will be sure
she has glimpsed a rare white elephant

in the jungle, though it was night,
and her own pale hand
pressed against the glass like an ear.

IN THE GARDEN

In the third month of my dog's illness
I am dreaming about diamonds.
Intruders have come to take the family home,
and I know I must hide the jewelry
somewhere on my person. Four platinum
and square diamond bracelets, one each for my siblings and me,
must disappear into my clothes.
One settles comfortably into the space between my breasts.
The others are more difficult—my socks,
bunched at the ankles? Under a braid in my hair?
No pockets—too obvious. In my underpants,
discomfort surely visible to even the most polite
looter? And when the door opens, I know
I will most surely lose them all, my own
and my family's precious future, betrayed
when the most privately hidden
slips down my pant leg to the floor.

Last night my good red dog
twitched and pawed in his first seizure.
Today he wanders the house, tripping
over every obstacle and bumping lightly
against every doorframe he passes. He finds himself
in corners, apparently baffled. But he can catch
a tennis ball bounced off the floor,
something he never did before. I am not saying
he received a gift for what he has lost—every
trick in the world would not replace
his lost grace. He has been for seven years
my light-footed one, living
more in the air than on the ground,
a fine dancer in any green world.

Most other nightmares I had in his life
were unsubtle fears for him—his yard

broken out of, cars menacing, or a wrongdoer
I would often wake myself up punching. None
prepared me for this diminishing, this unfocussed
wrongness like a gray moth behind his eyes.

In the February weather I patrol my yard,
freeing new daffodils from last winter's leaves
only to want protection for them again
in the white morning. I read garden books and plan
a blooming paradise for spring. I know now
where to hide those things
I cannot do without.
The platinum and diamond dream bracelets,
the musky gardenia my lover gave me,
the bright eyes of my delicate burnished dog,
I will bury in the dark earth and
watch over them like a sun.

SLEEP

He is jealous of the pillow she lays her head on.
It is the way she thinks about it, in the afternoon, with a longing
so near to lust.
At night at least
he is with her there, but he doesn't feel the pleasure
she knows when she is relieved from that terrible burden,
her body.

He watches her for signs of infidelity. If just once she turned down
that great black abyss for his sake,
perhaps there was hope. He might even be winning.
She announces her intention to nap and he cries, "No!" But her eyes
are already there. She wants that slow, inevitable escape. She must
have it. Only the cry
of her dog would keep her from it,
and then, later, she'd have to return again
to find her way in that familiar wood.
She talks about it like that—a wood, with dark trees, sweet flowers, and
      strange animals
drawing close, then bounding away.

Sometimes she tells him her dreams. Astonished,
he sees the apocalypse come a hundred ways; he sees her family
in the most embarrassing poses. Sometimes he awakens her
in the dim light of nightlights
whimpering and thrashing in the bed beside him.
The nightmare is always a dog lost or hurt,
the one tragedy she cannot bear.

He brings her feathers,
red and blue, striped and iridescent,
and she tells him the birds who lost them.
He wants to give her
the flight she has in her best dreams.

Nothing in his previous life could have prepared him
for this necessary giving over of his lover.
Sometimes in the morning she is still tired,
as from a long walk. He watches her gulp water
and push her hair back from her face. Sometimes he swears
there are twigs and leaves in her hair then. Sometimes he closes his eyes
    again,
trying to find that lost wood and follow her tracks,
but he never does,
and she can't tell him the way.

AFTER WATCHING A COLIN FIRTH MOVIE, I THINK ABOUT QUANTUM MECHANICS

> *From the many worlds viewpoint, the universe is like a tree
> that branches and re-branches into myriads of new sub-
> branches with every passing picosecond.*
>
> —John Cramer

*I know we are lovers
in some alternate reality,* I think, though
of course I do not know if we are, or if,
knowing him that way in another world, I would tell myself
I am better off in this one. And I remember
when I fed our dogs a second dinner
in the late evening, habit guiding me
to pick up the bowls and fill them with hard,
dry food, and then went back out
to the living room and sat down beside
my husband, who said, "Did you just
feed the dogs?" I said, "No," looked at
the tv, and then cried, "Wait!" as if to stop the five-minute-old
me from carrying out this stupidity. I think my track
of routine intersected with another track from one of those
myriad other worlds in which I'd made some other decision
perhaps as recently as that morning, and put on the black
socks instead of the brown ones, which somehow led
to me getting home late and feeding my beloveds five hours
after their usual time. I would like to explain
how I do things without consciousness, the way,
driving, I find myself home with no memory
of any turns, or, after a stop sign, wondering
if I did actually stop, or just blew through
oblivious, lucky no other drivers
moved temporarily through worlds where they
had no stop sign, worlds where our straight roads
turn on themselves, where voices call out
to negate our silences, and kisses

tumble from the sky like ripe plums,
sweet, soft orbs that have no idea
whether they're falling into this world or the next.

WHAT THE MRI DOESN'T SHOW

On the phone my sister says
she's stuck in all directions,
and I imagine a starfish cursed
with a mind in each leg
and no desire the same.
But that's not quite accurate—
it's more like some winged thing
held in place with glue,
and that glue is her injured
brain, shaken inside the skull
three times like a ripe peach
in a glass jar.
            The first time
she was sixteen and jumping
the horse I loved best;
he could not help
that she was under
him when he fell. So much of
what we said was just who she was—
late, disorganized, messy,
no sense of direction—
may be no more an inherent part
of her personality than having three legs
is the natural form of the cat
my father's girlfriend adopted.
I don't know, though I was nine
when it happened and should
remember.
            The others
were this past year, two car accidents
in the ice of a Boulder winter.
For a while she carried her mail
around in her purse,
unable to decide what she should do
about the bills, bank statements,

solicitations for money and sympathy.
Sounds hit her like fists. Complex
visual patterns—paisley or traffic—become nets
to entangle her. But when she sends
me a letter to edit for her
the clear, thoughtful prose sweeps
me up, her deep compassion a throbbing
rhythm under the leggiero phrasing,
and I realize how fine an instrument
she still has, and enough music
to save or break
her into pieces, trying to get out.

GREETING

Drive down a lightly graveled road
between a field of corn and a field of soybeans.
Turn off the engine. Open
the windows. This is very important.
How else can you
smell the purple clover?
Your life is a tree
in all this open space.
And the birds—
sparrows and red-winged blackbirds, robins,
mourning doves, swallows—
they do not need your life.
This is a good
thing. You are lonely enough
for yourself to bear.
It is June.
Stay until the corn
is so tall a child could
walk into it and disappear.
It will not seem like
a long wait.
Look at the sky, the silver shapes
going about their own
stately business.
When you
walk out of the whispering corn
you will get into the car,
sit in front of the steering wheel.
You will wonder how you got
old enough to drive, big
enough to reach the pedals.
Smile in greeting. Tell yourself to
smell the clover, watch the birds.

Tell yourself welcome.
Tell yourself
all the stories you know.

My Father's Shirt

The drunk ex-husband
of my father's girlfriend died
in his bed in his double-wide trailer
after having sex with the neighbor woman.
She was already gone, so we
don't have to worry about her.
Days later

my father's girlfriend
had to drive her ex-mother-in-law to the funeral home,
relay questions about open or closed casket, music and eulogies
to the ancient woman at a shout. There was
nobody else. The old drunk ex-husband (we'll call him
the old drunk from now on,
which may get confusing because my father
was once a drunk, too, though he quit
cold turkey years ago)
apparently couldn't hold on
to anybody, even his youngest daughter,
who at age six was smothered under him for hours
when he passed out and fell onto her. (No indication
of anything sexual, so we can be relieved
on that point, too.) Anyway

the old drunk was in life a genius, something like
40 points above normal in the IQ department,
though he slaved away as a lab rat for years
because he never finished college
and pissed off every boss he ever had. He was
by this time enjoying retirement, though, the plan for which
was to go down to the VFW hall and drink
with other men all day until it was time to be driven home,
watch late night tv, and slobber into bed. And we should care nothing

for this old drunk and his pathetic habits except
for this last part, concerning my father, a dependable man
the ex had never met, which is
that he had an old suit his daughter found rumpled
in the trailer's closet but
no dress shirt to go with it, and so
he went into the coffin and then
into the ground wearing
my father's white shirt.

THE FLYING TOOTHBRUSHES

was not the name of my mother's intramural volleyball team,
but her team—the Shoehorns—played against them in 1956,

when my mother was a sorority girl
who didn't need any other nickname than the one her parents gave her—

Dinny, a fun, pillow-fight-and-practical-joke name
for a girl who made friends by listening.

She played field hockey and basketball, too, her awkwardness
falling away in sport. She tried to teach me the hook shot

that won her game after game in her all-girl high school, but I couldn't
shoot to save any life. On the next page in her scrapbook, a poem

from my father asking when she would come with him to Dunkirk
again, and on the next page, a letter from her brother saying their

mother would get over her disapproval, it was just such a shock,
she and my father being so young, not even twenty-one. My mother

and I look at the page, read the letter. We do not have to speak
of the years my father's anger ruled her, the recompense of four children.

When my father comes over from his house across town for dinner,
she says, "You have to see this." Side by side on the couch,

they look at the poem, laugh over her limerick response ending
with "supurfluous," misspelled and not rhyming with anything.

The time between then and now is a hard edge they threw themselves
against over and over. I look at them and do not say, "Don't turn

the page." Somewhere in the split atoms of the air girlish laughter echoes
like it's found the polished wood surface of a gym floor and bounced.

Somewhere The Flying Toothbrushes are circling, a carefree tribe
of witches, magicking the past into a swirl of unbound images:

here, she lives in the loving cage of her upper class family;
here she is a girl among other girls, not knowing she should have stayed

in their company, they always were
her heart's desire; here, she meets my father, and begins that

long journey; here she is sixty-six, and ready to claim
what she loves at last.

WHIPPOORWILL

When I lie down to sleep in the late afternoon
or step shivering from a warm shower

sometimes I don't recognize my house,
my towels, my Chinese quilt, my own

oversized and sluggish body, the flowers
days past spent and still drowning

in a vase on my fake wood-grain countertop.
I close my eyes, sure I will awake/emerge

in my real house, the moss green 1970 two-story
where my mother waits to put my hair into ponytails

swinging from the sides of my head
before we walk out into the summer dusk

to pick raspberries (in spite of the praying mantises),
until on the path in our backyard she stops,

says, "Listen. That's a whippoorwill,"
and the name of that onomatopoeic bird

pushes out of my mouth in a rush
of feathers. I open my eyes.

FLATLAND

The wind is right sometimes…
—Nick Mazzeo

The language of wind
is foreign, full
of wispy consonants
designed for a subtler
tongue than ours (we who are afraid
of our own sibilance)
and needing everything in the world
to make its sound.
But when I listen
to the wind where I was born
I hear something
almost ready to sort itself
into meaning, and I
am caught in that moment between
someone saying something unexpected and half-heard
and my translation
of the jumbled
syllables. If I could just stay
here forever in the flatland
of Illinois maybe
I would find my life.

IV

CELESTIAL MADNESS

Mars came closer
to Earth this summer
than it has for 60,000 years, or will again
for another 284.
And my father's mind—green
and hilly like the part of Pennsylvania
he came from—was engulfed
by higher and higher tidal waves,
inexplicably far inland, driving him up
and up the rocky slopes until the water lapped
at his toes, until his checked shirt
was wet at the elbows, until land
fell out from under him and he was swept
away.
      Now he's flailing out there, convinced
he's lost all of his money and more,
warning the entire family of our financial ruin.
And I am afraid
of it all—that the drugs
they are giving him will prove no
raft for him to cling to,
that he will not recognize the shape
of distant reality when he sees it,
that he will not remember
how to swim, and when he sinks,
the mermaids (whose tails will be made
of glittering coins)
will not be kind to him.

WITNESS

My student says, *This backpack*
feels like being pregnant in the back,
as she tries to squeeze out my office door without
knocking over anything. She tells me
about a time when she was pregnant
in the usual way
and she parked in too narrow a space at the mall.
She could not get out of the car. Finally
she had to give up and drive away.
But the reason she remembers it so vividly
is because there was a man sitting in a car
nearby, a car filled with the paraphernalia of
children, watching her and laughing.
I laugh, too, and she
smiles, and hands me a piece of paper,
and leaves.
                    Inside I find
sympathy for me in the time of my father's madness,
which I blurted to her after class
the day after a torturous Thanksgiving break,
tales of *her* father's depression,
her mother's mother's delusions, and a confession:
she is bipolar. This lovely woman suffers
and still clips articles for me and her classmates
related to anything we might have mentioned in class,
she has weather inside I can only glimpse.
And the other things
I know about her make sense: the o.d. last time
she was in college,
her great concern for her perfectionist son,
her shaky hands in conference, from allergy medicine
she told me the first time.
And like that, we are bonded,
one of us standing in a cramped office
smelling of old paper and dust, the other

tramping off down the hallway carrying enough on her back
to make another life—her own, from hairdresser
to schoolteacher—two women
witness to each other's sorrow.
And I don't know why, but I feel
lighter, I feel
like laughing.

INSOMNIAC IN THE AFTERNOON

I'm shaky and frenzied from lack of sleep, hungry
in unpredictable ravenous fits and too tired to
remember to stop eating when I'm full, popping

candy into my mouth until it's gone, wondering
if I tasted it at all. As if that affects
the body's crimson process, chocolate turned

soon and easily to indiscriminate sugar
sliding down glistening interior tubes
in a hyperactive tide.

I hate what my mind does
when it's like this, neither penned
behind fences of housework, appointments, routine

nor loosed into the open fields of a
book, a walk, a languid afternoon with dogs.
Self is such a sloppy amalgam,

most of the parts fixated on all the wrong things:
what moves, what's stuck,
what minutiae must be managed

for it all to start over again.
My friend tells me my to do list
is a poem, and I cough

out a laugh, "Fucking depressing
poem." I want my poems
like I want my life:

prisms neatly taking apart light
and making it whole again, scales
measured out in random perfection

by wind chimes dangling from a red-leaved tree,
soft, shy pleasure of clean sheets
to still the generations of my loss.

VIRID

Green is the thread I'm hanging by.

Green is my fast-beating heart when the wind's coming up and the whole world is movement.

In a dark green place I can lie down and sleep and sleep and sleep.

Green is conversation on the page, my words telling those black letters about the sky.

My father's eyes are green, except when I'm angry with him. Then they're hazel.

I grew up in a green house on sixteen acres of pasture. I found four-leaf clovers in the yard whenever I looked hard enough.

Fireflies are gold-green pulsing constellations over the fields in July.

All the myth I love—faeries that might snatch away an unsuspecting child (how often lying under the open window I feigned innocent helplessness) and people turning to seals and the magic of sea and stones—comes from the Emerald Isle. Yeats and his music comes from there.

Ponds and creeks and even small rivers are filled with green water.

Colorado sage has so much blue and gray you can hardly see the green, but you can smell it.

I've never lived anyplace that was green all year round.

In the summer, green is lavish.

Laughing, you turn to me
and pull a leaf from my hair.

LIVING IN THE FUTURE

I'm in the Detroit airport walking fast and alone
towards my gate—I'm going home
for Christmas, though home isn't
so much anymore since my father lost
himself in dark corridors of worry—
and suddenly I'm inside
a colored tube, riding a moving sidewalk and
listening to tinkling music while pink
and blue and green slide across walls and ceilings
behind continent-shaped silvery glass cutouts
so smooth they seem liquid. It's a dream of the future
I would have had 25 years ago,
light and sound and movement,
everything but the personal flying machines I just knew
would be common one day, at least
by the year 2000 (so round a number;
I rolled *millennium* on my tongue
for weeks after I learned the word).
The colors and the waterfall music soothe me.
I have two hours between the plane
that left me here and the one
that will take me to family, so when I stumble
off at the end of my ride (I'm always
slow to adjust speeds) I turn
and get on the rolling floor going back.
This time I feel like I'm in a garden
and I even close my eyes, only to be
brushed by someone hurrying past with a wheeled
suitcase and clicking heels. When I open my eyes
I feel even calmer; I am going away from my father
and the sad maelstrom of his disease,
I am traveling this giant esophagus
back towards the mouth, I am a ten-year-old girl
happy to abandon everything familiar
for this sleek, multi-colored sky.

SYMPHONY

The tree flowers white—snow
on every cupped branch end
stuns me in this
March storm, how perfectly
the tree is shaped, how it sings
its chilly beauty even
to me, on this charcoal street,
full of my own mournful & nervous
songs. I think of other flowerings:
white cranes behind an air-conditioned house
in urban Bangkok, bright crimson speck
of beetle on a shiny evergreen leaf,
and, when I was five, waking
after a fall from a willow to
the worried faces of the neighbors' Great Danes
hanging over me like helpless uncles—
how soft they were
under my fingers,
and how warm.

THIS MORNING I READ ABOUT THE STRANGLED GIRL

It took me all these years
to figure out it's turning
away from the furry hump beside the road,
hunching my shoulders,
that makes the small life ended in
pain turn to a stone
in my stomach.

I am filled
with stones.

Today I will try
to stand up
and let these small and large
hurts pierce me. Sorrow
of the lost child, of the one
who has lost her, arrows
that rend me again
and again, let them come.
Despair of the
chickadee I found dead
in my screened-in porch,
guilt of the girl whose newly ex-
girlfriend leapt from a bridge,
rage of my father hammering
my sweet, joyous brother into
the shape of a man,
let them come.
　　　　　　　Let my eyes
burn dry. Let my body
open like a wound.

on the first day of the Year of the Monkey it looks like
some kind of arctic apocalypse, the wind
blowing snow across the road in front of us
so for a few sharp seconds it's like being
blind, the individual flakes swirling pinpricks
of light on eyes wide open and staring,
looking for some kind of landmark and not
the grill of a Mack truck coming straight
at us as we fear. I'm thinking
of the ice storms of my childhood, board games
by candlelight and a fire in the fireplace and icicles
melting in the gas oven for water.
How I loved those slowed-down days,
no tv no homework no errands no one
running off to do better things with
more interesting people, and then one day the sun
striking off ice everywhere like organ music
until the wires tying us to duty and routine
emerged from their shells of ice and life
started up again.
                    The thing about apocalypse is
you feel proud just to survive,
the vaguely guilty pleasures of food and company
just pleasures, because what else could you do
anyway? A trip to the hardware store
for the right fasteners to put up a shelf
that's been sitting idly in the garage for months?
The research on insurance (can you pay
a little less per month for coverage almost
as good)? That dentist appointment you've been
meaning to make? So when we pull up
in front of Lucky City I'm just happy
to have made it, to have missed
disaster, to see in the snow and wind something
real to be afraid of and grateful to,

and I feel a kind of love for the terrible
winter weather, the kind of love that has driven
humans for millennia to kneel down,
offer sacrifice, bow their heads and pray
so wind and rain and earth and sky
might have mercy on us in our pitiful lives.

AUTUMN BIRTHDAY

—with thanks to Dorothy Barresi for the final lines

At thirty-five a woman holds
the handle of a shovel like a staff. She knows
what to carry in her purse for an afternoon
or a whole day's excursion. She is known
and, often, wants to be. She leaves
behind her as she walks
a hollow place in the air, gateway
to worlds in which she runs marathons, lives
barefoot by the sea, sells her heart
for a thousand jewels bedecking her skin like butterflies
or a boy's too-pretty face.
This is the year
she recognizes age is a sword.
She shrugs.
It's a big heaven.
Anything can happen.

AFTERNOON

All we need
hovers before us
a dream of gold
wheat and sky
shimmering warm (but
what kind of pass
do you need to get
into a place like that?
we wonder, fumbling
in pockets and muttering sorry
as though the cashier waited
impatiently, popping
her gum).

All we need
is entrance into
serenity and if
we find it in a deserted
movie theater who
can blame us?

Need is
a lion waiting
by the front door,
a sun going
down to the other world.
Hold me, we say.
We say, let me go.
Need is not the leaf
carried miles on the
surface of the water.
It is, of course,
the water.

V

How to Fix Your Sister's 110-Year-Old House
in Ivesdale, Illinois

1. Drive twenty miles out into the cornfields. Take roads marked by numbers or not at all, roads that run straight along the imaginary lines of latitude and longitude, though you will see no curve here in the flatlands of your origin.

1. Stare out the car window across harvested fields, at the brown earth and the gigantic blue sky and the islands of farmhouses on their rafts of green grass with great tree-masts breasting the wind. Look and look until your eyes are dry, and wet, and dry again. Look as if you knew you were going blind or to prison or to Mars or to the moody, tree-shrouded East tomorrow and forever.

1. Your conveyance—car or ship—will roll in the swells, will chase the sun's fleet reflection. Do not be tempted to trail your hand along the surface like a child on a hot day. These waters are more dangerous than the Lethe; they are not forgetfulness, but memory.

1. Remember—because you cannot help it—you were born here, you are of here. Sometimes you feel like Hawaii's volcanic rock, not to be taken away lest disaster come. Sometimes you feel if you open your mouth to speak only cornflowers will come out, whole sentences of Osage oranges, fireflies, Tiger lilies, Queen Anne's lace, whippoor-will. Grammar and syntax of horizontal lines, horizons, space.

1. Breathe.

1. Breathe.

1. Breathe.

MOTH

I go to the muddy banks of the Sangamon
over and over again, like a tongue
goes to the hole where a tooth once was or a thumb
slips perfectly into a child's mouth—strange

human thing, universally
soothing. I go because those banks
were close to the edge of my childhood country
and that boundary feels familiar but not
to the heart. Close to the bright flame
of the house and barn and yard I loved so much I still
dream about it, awake and asleep, but not
so close I'm blinded, or burned.

THE NOT-KNOWING

My foolish dogs run
out into the back yard
at night. They don't know
it's dangerous here—
snakes dripping from the oaks
like Spanish moss
and alligators, eyes glittering, threading
their way through the suburban
neighborhood. I think my fence will
keep out the bad things but what do I know
of Florida's prehistoric monsters, its poisonous
frogs, its flaming ants and femme fatale spiders
vicious and thrifty enough to kill
everything I love in one terrible crash
of coincidence and pandemonium?

And so I chase
after them, their barking and my frightened
calling surely waking the early-to-bed,
early-to-rise neighbors. The grass
is as sharp under my feet as emeralds.
I rattle the box of dog treats with its photograph
of a happy and well-trained puppy
and in that moment before I hear the jingle
of dog tags coming towards me I am caught
again in other moments of not-knowing:

the flooded bottomland with my neck
stretched to keep my chin above water, before
my mother walked out in her clothes to save me;

the back of a horse bent
on home and fast
as a striking heron;

the whisper
of my curious thumb sliding across the axe blade
and the surprise of cranberry blood
beading from the cut.

ENVOI

Colors in paintings—the canvas exhaling
royal blues and swaths of red, edges always touching
like too much food on a plate at a buffet—
are not like experience because there's never
enough gray,
                 gray sky, water, concrete, gray air
between figures in the foreground. Oh let me
gorge myself on color, an impressionist binge.
Let my soft mother, poised to dive headlong
into the swift stream of her illness,
be distracted a moment by the rising
yellows and greens, the heady pinks.
Let her pause there, the coming dark a mere smudge
in the background. (The falling lights,
the blind future.) Let someone paint that.

GLITTER

Belief in the wind waxes and wanes in me, white shirts billowing
in empty abandon, leaves carrying messages of damage
somewhere else.

Call me, my best friend said, *the instant you hear her diagnosis.* But I didn't.
    Bad
news is too hard to share.

And my pallid talent now is to tend my grief,
chop chop with a hoe and water relentlessly and wonder
if growth is always a good
thing. Maybe it's a vineyard, the final
product resembling the fresh as a canoe
resembles a baby, little boat
of mothers' dreams.

I wanted you so much. The others, I didn't care whether they were boys or girls.
    But you,
you were my little girl, my mother said every October.

And even as a child, what I wanted
was childhood, my green blanket
that smelled of her. Safe as triumph. And now?
The shirt of hers I cannot wear, but hold
to my face once a month. Recipes
for failure, recipes for loss. Dying
breezes and pollen that falls, suddenly unsuspended,
like glitter.

AFTER BOTH MY PARENTS ARE DEAD

I dream, again, that my sister and I
buy our old house in the country: four
bedrooms, sixteen acres, eight-stall barn. This
time what is different
is that the previous owners left it
unfinished, half-restored, and the floors
in all the upstairs rooms have holes, nothingness

where our feet should go, and though we lie
down in the solid places trying
to be happy this home is ours again
we cannot sleep for fear of falling in the night
and the insidious worry
that we have made a bad
investment, that we cannot fix
what is lost and broken, we cannot
live here anymore.

LOST

Through fields of swaying grasses
that bloom and rise   a dark flock
under monuments laughing in the earth and seeping salt
we ride in tiny open cars, in baskets, on sleds, on
horseback   We navigate
gray treescapes catching ghosts in our hands
(they glow like fireflies) and still
we rove   we move   always moving

because sometimes a whisper crawls
towards us   a tendril curling and grasping
prehensile   It carries red stones on its tongue
It speaks of all
we have given away   all we have yet
to know
and we want
to ask it questions   to listen at night
our foreheads pressed to cold
windows

We want
nothing that we have   We
want to stop   We want to
arrive at the green river
where someone familiar will take us by the elbow
and help us board the glittering barge

ACKNOWLEDGMENTS

My deepest gratitude to the many people who contributed suggestions, support and inspiration, including Ira Sukrungruang, Carolyn Alessio, Dorey Riegel, the Poetry Gals of Oswego, the Prose Boys of Oswego, my family, my teachers, and my students.

Grateful acknowledgment is made to the following publications in which these poems appeared, sometimes in slightly different forms:

88—"Geography"
The Baltimore Review—"Celestial Madness"
The Barely South Review—"Naga"
Bellevue Literary Review—"What the MRI Doesn't Show"
Cimarron Review—"In the Garden"
Connecticut Review—"And of the Silent Hero"
Crazyhorse—"Ambrosia"
Epiphany—"What I Knew"
failbetter.com—"Autumn Birthday," "Childhood: A Portrait"
Louisiana Literature—"Die Fledermaus"
The Melic Review—"Sleep"
Poetry Kanto—"Afternoon," "Symphony," "Whippoorwill"
The Sycamore Review—"The Anger Suit"
West Branch—"Driving Into Oswego for Chinese Food," "Prayer to
    Buddha for a Good Journey"

Special recognition: *Castaway* by Katherine Riegel was one of four finalists for the 2010 FutureCycle Poetry Book Prize.

Book design: Cover art by Tandi Venter © 2010, tandiventer.com; cover design and typography by Diane Kistner (dkistner@futurecycle.org), Calisto body type and titling.

The FutureCycle Poetry Book Prize

FutureCycle Press conducts an annual full-length poetry book competition open to any poet writing in the English language. The winning manuscript is normally published over the summer, with the poet receiving a $1,000 prize plus 25 copies of the published book. Finalists may also be offered publishing contracts. Submissions of book manuscripts are accepted from January 1 to March 31 each year for that year's prize. The press also publishes individual poems in its online magazine, *FutureCycle Poetry*. These poems, which remain online indefinitely, are collected into an annual print edition each November.

To be considered, all submissions must be received via our online submission form. To avoid unnecessary delays or unread returns of submitted work, poets should review our guidelines:

www.futurecycle.org/guidelines.aspx

Poetry Books from FutureCycle Press

FutureCycle Poetry Book Prize Winners
Stealing Hymnals from the Choir by Timothy Martin (2010)
No Loneliness by Temple Cone (2009)

FutureCycle Poetry Book Prize Finalists
Castaway by Katherine Riegel (2010 Finalist)
Simple Weight by Tania Runyan (2010 Finalist)
Luminous Dream by Wally Swist (2010 Finalist)
Beyond the Bones by Neil Carpathios (2009 Finalist)

Full-length Books
The Porous Desert by David Chorlton
Violet Transparent by Anne Coray

Chapbooks
The Secret Life of Hardware by Cheryl Lachowski
Colma by John Laue
Scything by Joanne Lowery
A Love Letter to Say There Is No Love by Maria Russell-Williams

www.ingramcontent.com/pod-product-compliance
Lightning Source LLC
Chambersburg PA
CBHW070041110426
42741CB00036B/3113